NATURE'S NOT SCARY

Nature's not scary

6 nature walks to take with kids under 7

RACHEL ABEL

Wildkids Australia

Copyright © 2022 by Rachel Abel, Wildkids Australia

All rights reserved. No part of this publication may be reproduced, distributed or transmitted in any form or by any means, including photocopying, recording, or other electronic or mechanical methods, without the prior written permission of the publisher, except in the case of brief quotations embodied in critical reviews and certain other noncommercial uses permitted by copyright law.

First Printing, 2022

For permission requests, write to the author at: wildkidsaustralia@gmail.com

Rachel Abel
Wildkids Australia
www.wildkidsaustralia.com.au

Ordering Information:
Quantity sales. Special discounts are available on quantity purchases by corporations, associations, and others. For details, contact "Special Sales" at the address above.
Nature's not scary: 6 nature adventure walks to take with kids under 7/Rachel Abel — 1st ed.
ISBN 978-0-6455838-0-9
ISBN 978-0-6455838-1-6 (Ebook)

Cover design and illustrations by Stacey Benson Design

CONTENTS

Dedication	vi
Disclaimer	vii
Acknowledgements	ix
Introduction	xi
How to use this book	xv
Plan your adventure	xvii

1	WALK ONE	1
2	WALK TWO	7
3	WALK THREE	13
4	WALK FOUR	20
5	WALK FIVE	27
6	WALK SIX	33

Nature Journal Pages	41
Make you own observation kit	53
Risk assessment	57

Dedicated to my husband (aka Wildkids Trevor) for being the most wonderful marriage and business partner! To our children, Alex and Pirran for enjoying so many nature adventures together.

And to all the parents, carers and kids who I hope will make some memories together with this book as a guide.

DISCLAIMER

This book provides information and inspiration to support you in getting out and about in nature. It will include tips and advice for making adventures in nature as safe as possible, but it's no substitution for carrying out your own risk assessment. Tips will be included on how to do that too!

ACKNOWLEDGEMENTS

I'd like to acknowledge the traditional custodians of the land, the Dharug people, on whose land I live and have gratefully walked in writing this book. To show my respect to elders past and present. And to extend that respect to the first nations people of Australia who generously share their knowledge and encourage us to take care of mother earth.

A heartfelt thank you to all the people who helped make this book possible...

To all the educators and parents in our community who have been on Wildkids adventures with us.

To our local business community including the Better Business Partnership, The Home Show and others.

To our worldwide online business community, who have supported us through growing our business to reach a wider audience online than we ever could have dreamed possible.

To our family and friends who have cheered us on every step of the way.

To Alexandra Franzen and Lindsay Smith for sharing their writing and publishing know-how.

And to Stacey Benson @staceybensondesign for the wonderful artwork.

INTRODUCTION

6 nature walk adventures to take with kids under 7

For the anxious, adventurous and anyone in between no matter where you live.

Why I wrote this book for you

Last year we were running some activities at an expo, meeting hundreds of families and kids and introducing them to what we do at Wildkids Australia. One family stuck in my mind more than the others.

Just so you know, my husband and business partner aka 'Wildkids Trevor' is just brilliant at engaging kids with nature. His enthusiasm draws them in. They look at him with wide-eyed wonder as he bounces around exclaiming how 'plants are clever' or getting his hands amongst the dirt and talking about composting.

But not all kids are super comfortable up close with bugs, bark, leaves or anything new or mucky. The truth is that for some, nature is scary. One particular kid we met who was about 4 years old was so shy. They were literally hiding behind their Mum as they watched their older sibling step forward confidently to touch a piece of old termite nest.

Trevor encouraged the Mum to hold the piece too. At this point, I saw the younger child look up and decide that if Mum could do it, well then they could do it too. The look of pride and accomplishment on this child's face when they plucked up the courage to put the gnarly piece of nest in their hands was so inspiring. I got a little choked up. As did the Mum, who admitted to me quietly that she had always been terrified of nature but was desperate to make sure she didn't pass that on to her family. She just didn't really know where to start because it had not been something in her childhood experience.

I connected with how she was feeling because both of our kids have anxiety. We've been careful to gently support them in developing a more adventurous spirit, building on their innate curiosity. Gently expanding their horizons rather than throwing them in the deep end. We've witnessed them take those experiences into other aspects of their lives. Often in families, there are one or more parents or kids who love taking risks, getting muddy, climbing a tree and others who feel more apprehensive. I wrote this book with that in mind.

"It's super simple" one of the pre-schoolers announced during a Wild-kids session.

What is?" Trevor asked

"Looking after everything" they replied

"Why do you think that?"

"Well, if you like somebody or something, you are kind to it and look after it. So, all you have to do is be kind to the thing you like. Then that would mean that everybody will be kind to what they like."

"What do you like?"

"Um...I like flowers and I like rabbits and I like birds but not cockroaches and bugs" they said.

"What if birds ate cockroaches and bugs and the flowers needed the bugs to pollinate?"

"Does that mean that I have to be nice to them if the birds eat them?

"Probably"

"Well, maybe you've just got to be kind to everything then."

Encouraging children to enjoy adventures in nature and having good conversations about what's around them will gradually bring them to find nature to be less scary. Their lives will be richer for it. Spending time playing outdoors increases emotional well-being, builds self-esteem and supports creativity. Plus, the connection with nature introduces children at a young

age to the concepts of conservation and sustainability. You are so much more likely to care for something if you enjoy it, know it and view it as important. Together we're raising and educating the next generation of eco-protectors.

HOW TO USE THIS BOOK

This book is written so that each adventure can be adapted to wherever you live - city, beach or woods. Anywhere really. You choose where to take the walks. Around the corner on your block, on a trip to the local park or on a day trip further away.

I know that as a busy parent or educator, coming up with new interesting activities can be exhausting. So I've planned everything out in 6 walks for you, with 3 key activities per walk and step-by-step instructions on what to take with you and where to go. Each walk centres around a different nature and sustainability learning theme with suggested questions to spark conversations.

For each walk, I've also created a downloadable activity sheet for you to take with you on your phone, tablet or as a printout (on recycled paper of course! You can download all of the activity packs for this book at: www.wildkidsaustralia.com.au/naturesnotscary

Dip in and out of the walks in any order. Take the same favourite walk in different locations. Be inspired to plan your own and include it in the blank section at the end.

There are nature journal pages for each walk so you can record your memories. With spaces to draw, stick or press little things you find. Download extra journal pages at: www.wildkidsaustralia.com.au/naturesnotscary

This book is also perfect if you are an educator looking for structured nature learning resources to help plan activities. Who maybe wants to inspire their communities to get involved with sustainability at home.

If you are an anxious parent or have anxious kids, this book will support you in taking those first adventures together and creating beautiful memories. And if your kids are already adventurous, it will give you some fresh ideas to extend the learning that's possible.

I would love for you to send me pictures of this book covered in dirt and mud, scribbled in and with curled-up edges. This book is designed as a field guide so please take it out into the field, onto the pavement or through the forest.

Extra resources

I am a total science nerd and we know from the research that making connections with the natural world has benefits in stimulating curiosity, discovery and an early understanding of biodiversity. There is also growing evidence that spending time playing outdoors increases focused attention and emotional well-being. It builds confidence and self-esteem as well as supports creativity. If you are interested in learning more, head to the additional resources section at the end of this book.

PLAN YOUR ADVENTURE

All of the walks in this book are flexible. You can enjoy them in a local area that you know well or choose to experience them on a day trip or holiday to a new place.

You don't need to walk very far. A shorter walk can be better for younger kids. Take time to explore what's along the way. Walking around the block, and noticing everything around you can easily take an hour with a toddler. Spotting ants walking in a line or a spider wrapping up a fly will be just as thrilling as a frog or rabbit.

Experiment with taking the same walk at different times of the day. The kinds of bugs and birds that are about in the morning may be quite different to those at dusk. At midday, the light can be completely different to the evening. Even though younger children may be tired there is something extra exciting about being outside as it gets dark.

You'll need to decide what to take with you depending on where you go. Below I've suggested what you might like to have in your 'nature walk backpack'. Kids love the idea of a special backpack for nature exploring. Give them the job of helping to pack it and then check items every time you go out. It's fun to collect items over time, giving children the task of spotting equipment for the backpack. Keep your backpack packed and ready for your next adventure. Each walk has details about any additional items to add to the backpack for the different adventures.

Please don't feel you need to have everything listed to enjoy your walk. If you head out around the block with just a bottle of water, well, that's fine. And there is no need to buy new. We find most of our identification and reference books in second-hand bookshops. I love to recycle, reuse and repurpose. If you can make it or buy it second-hand, please do! In the 'Make your own observation kit' chapter, you'll find instructions for making your own bug viewer from household items.

Nature walk backpack

- Magnifying glass
- Binoculars
- Compass
- String
- Collecting jar or pot
- Paper sticky tape
- Water bottle
- Pocket-size identification and reference books - plants, animals, geology etc.
- Small first aid kit - sticking plasters, insect bite cream, compression bandage
- Bug viewer and/or pooter (see page xxx for instructions to make your own)
- Pencils and notepad

You might also like to take

- Hat, raincoat, and sunscreen depending on the weather
- Clipboard - for the printable walk and activity pages

- Penknife
- Map
- Camera or phone

Things to remember...

Do your risk assessment of the area you will be walking in. See the 'risk assessment' chapter in this book for a quick guide.

Dress for the area and weather. Closed-in, sturdy shoes are always best for nature hikes. They will protect feet from sharp sticks, stones, or insect bites and will be comfortable. If you're going on a long walk, pack some layers so you can take clothing off or put on, depending on the temperatures and conditions that day.

Always check the information signs for any area you are exploring. They will contain important notes about whether there is a special conservation area with particular rules and any wildlife to look out for.

If you want to turn over a rock or log to see what's underneath, turn it towards you so that anything bitey or stingy can run away from you. Keep fingers out of the way. Use a stick rather than your hand to move things aside gently. Check what's there before inviting children to look more closely. Always put everything back as you found it, so any creatures are not disturbed.

Please don't pick native plants that are growing. Take a photo or draw a picture instead!

If you would like to press some plants or flowers or stick something in your journal pages, it is OK to pick up something that has fallen unless there are conservation rules for that area.

Don't eat or touch what you cannot 100% identify.

Take a map and printed walk guide with you if you walk in an area with little or no mobile signal.

Please take care around water and don't leave children unsupervised. Ponds, streams and lakes can be fascinating wildlife areas but require extra caution.

Be ready for the children to make their own adventure! If they show no interest in the walk or activities you've planned, that's OK. It can be frustrating when we're excited and have put time into planning. However, giving kids the freedom to choose how they want to explore can be just as valuable and fun. Sometimes younger children might not be ready for a particular activity that they will love in 6 months. Come back to it another day or use the walks as a jumping-off point for their ideas.

Be matter of fact when talking with kids about risks. Kids are pretty good at risk assessment. As a parent and educator, you can decide what you need to let them know. Anxious kids tend to focus more on potential dangers. Let them take control of the conversation. Ask them to tell you what you might need to watch out for and what to do about it. And then ask them to suggest how best to avoid or deal with that situation.

Leave only footprints. Take all your rubbish with you.

| 1 |

WALK ONE

Sensory Scavenger Hunt

TIME: 30 MINUTES TO 2 HOURS
THEME: ADVENTURE
LOCATION: CITY, PARK, GARDEN, BEACH, WOODS

Kids love to explore. Heading off down a path first. Looking behind a tree. Playing hide and seek. There are many ways that children enjoy investigating the world around them. In this walk, we'll be tapping into that sense of adventure and engaging with nature using all of our available senses on a sensory scavenger hunt!

You don't need to live near a wild forest to find treasures on a sensory scavenger hunt.

Walking down the street or in your local park can bring just as much excitement to preschoolers. The warmth of tarmac in the sun, the splash of a muddy puddle, the buzz of insects, a soft breeze on the skin and the bright colours of flowers in gardens are special when we take time to enjoy them. As adults, we may have forgotten how interesting these experiences are for young children On this walk, we get the wonderful bonus of rediscovery.

We've created a fun activity pack for you to take along on your own sensory scavenger hunt - no matter where you live. Sensory play is crucial to early years development and can include anything that engages sight, smell, touch, hearing, taste as well as balance and coordination.

On a sensory walk in the woods you might smell the dampness of moss, balance on a fallen log, hear the sound of swashy grass and watch a sea eagle soaring overhead.

For kids who feel less confident getting out and about in nature, this sensory scavenger hunt builds familiarity in a comfortable setting. Start close to home with everyday found items. Give your child the job of looking after the activity sheet or ticking off the items that are spotted. Focus on items that feel good to touch or on sounds that are nice to hear. Gradually introduce different textures or smells. Plan walks in different locations as your child's confidence grows.

What you'll need

The sensory scavenger hunt activity pack
- download from wildkidsaustralia.com.au/naturesnotscary

Extra things to take with you in your nature adventure backpack:

- Paper - not too thick
- Crayons
- An old sauce bottle or similar
- Old jars for collecting

Sensory Scavenger Hunt - Snapshot

- Plan a walk that will take at least 30 minutes.
- Download the activity pack.
- The activity pack includes 3 sensory spotting sheets, one each for the city, woods or beach.
- Each sheet has pictures of things you might see, hear, smell or touch on a sensory walk.

- There is also an extra blank sheet for you to draw, stick in or write your own!
- Choose a sheet from the activity pack based on the kind of area where you'll be walking.
- Tick off each item you spot along the way.

Here are three simple ways to enjoy your nature-based sensory scavenger hunt.

1. **Stop for a while**

   When we are off exploring there is nothing better than running ahead to find the way or what's around the next bend in the track. If we stop for just a minute though we can take note of the smallest things around us. Try holding hands, and sitting or standing with your eyes closed in a safe spot. Notice the temperature and texture of the ground. How many sounds are around you? What kinds of smells are wafting about? Describe what you find on your sensory scavenger hunt activity sheet.

2. **Make some Natural musical instruments**

   Collect along your walk some large seeds, shells, leaves or anything else that might make a good sound. Using short lengths of string tie them onto a sturdy stick so that they will bash together when you shake them. You've made your own nature sounds rattle! Take along a clean empty bottle you can fill with whatever loose materials you find. Small pebbles, sand, bark or leaves make great sounds when popped into an old plastic sauce bottle with the lid closed. Be sure to make sure younger children can't open the lid unsupervised though.

3. **Make an impression**

   Once you've enjoyed ticking off what you find on your sensory scavenger hunt activity sheets, you can create your own multi-sensory adventure! Children will have fun deciding what they should record on their sheet (see the blank 'create your own' page in the activity pack). You might try rubbing some earth on the paper to see the colour it makes and feel the texture. Or stick in a feather, or leaf that you find. You could record a sound on your phone to play later. And take a copy of some bark patterns by holding a piece of paper onto a tree trunk and rubbing with a chunky crayon. Pop some damp leaves in a jar, or trap salty sea air to smell when you get back.

Conversation starters

When you're out and about on your scavenger hunt, there are so many conversations that we can centre around this activity.

- What do your ears do? Your eyes? Your nose?
- What does this leaf/twig/stone feel like? Does it have a smell?
- Can you taste the air?
- If you close your eyes, how many different sounds do you hear?
- Can animals smell us? Hear us?
- What is your favourite place outside? What does it sound, smell, feel like?
- How many different colours can you see?
- Can you find a smooth, bumpy or spiky thing?

Turn the page to add some notes to the journal space. There are some extra journal pages at the back of the book too.

What did I find today?

TODO IS ....

WHERE AM I?..

Draw something here

Draw a bug you saw

What can you smell?

What was the colour of the sky?

Stick a leaf here!

| 2 |

WALK TWO

Wild Things Spotting

TIME: 30 MINUTES TO 2 HOURS
THEME: FAUNA
LOCATION: PARK, STREET, GARDEN, BEACH, WOODS

Bugs are bug-tastic! Yes, they may be creepy, crawly, buzzy, stingy, slimy, sticky, bitey, swarmy, itchy and even stinky! But, bugs are also absolutely vital to the survival of everything on the planet. Without bugs and the important jobs they do we would have no food to eat, plants would have no soil to grow in. And waste and poo would build up in enormous mounds everywhere!

On this walk, we will explore the wonderful world of busy bugs.

Insects are a great focus for our wild things spotting walk. They are absolutely everywhere - except the ocean - and there is never a dull moment in the insect world. They move in interesting ways, have weird bodies and metamorphic lifecycles that make them great to observe. Children are intrigued by the variety of forms that insects take - from butterflies to beetles, to ants and mantids. There are also lots of other small invertebrates like worms, snails and slugs that make for intriguing minibeast spots.

For kids who may feel more nervous about bugs, give them the job of looking after the bug spotting activity sheet or your bug book so that they take charge of identifying each bug you find. Allow them to see how interested you are in each bug and that you are comfortable being close to bugs. Start with a slow snail and build up to spiders or quick-moving bugs. In time, their natural curiosity will take over and gradually they will forget to be worried.

What you'll need

The bug spotting activity pack

- download from wildkidsaustralia.com.au/naturesnotscary

Extra things to take with you in your nature adventure backpack:

- Insect identification book
- Clipboard
- Old jars for observing

Wild things spotting - snapshot

- Download the bug spotting activity pack.
- The activity pack includes a bug spotting guide with some commonly found bugs that are relatively easy to spot in most environments.
- There is also an extra blank sheet for you to draw or write your own!
- When you are planning your walk remember that a walk that usually takes 10 minutes will take at least 30 minutes when we are stopping to hunt for bugs!
- Take your time, walk slowly and look closely. Bugs might be hiding in all sorts of places. Check on the ground, in a bush, on tree bark, in the air around you.
- Look for signs of bugs like webs, nests or trails.
- Tick off each item you spot along the way.

Here are three simple ways to enjoy your wild things spotting walk.

1. **Turn over a rock**

    As well as the buzzy and flappy kind, so many little creatures live in quiet, secluded and damp spots. Turning over a rock can reveal tiny busy bug worlds that you may not have noticed before. Check the 'plan your adventure' chapter for notes on how to safely turn over rocks. You can experiment with different rocks in a variety of locations and conditions and discuss what's living under each. A damp spot in the forest, a dry area in the park or a stone in a pond or rockpool.

2. **Take a closer look**

   If you've found an interesting bug, try taking a closer look. If it's a slow-moving creature a magnifying glass held over it will reveal details of patterns, wings or antenna. You might catch a bug under a jar to give more time to identify and investigate it in detail. For small, quicker moving bugs a pooter is an ideal way to safely capture it. Full instructions on how to make and use a pooter are in the 'Make your own observation kit' chapter in this book. Once in the jar, you can use the magnification of the glass to get a closer look, identify it and perhaps draw it before releasing your bug back to its home.

3. **Create your own bug**

   Gather a few natural materials from your walk or from your garden to make a bug from natural materials when you get home. Use some natural play dough and string to create your own bug-like creatures. Perfect for younger children as a sensory activity and for older kids to engage their creativity and spark conversations about insects. We like to hang ours from a tree with some string so they fly about in the breeze! And when you've enjoyed your display the natural materials can be returned to where you collected them to become bug food.

Conversation starters

On your bug hunt or while you're making your own bug creatures, you might start some conversations about bugs with these questions.

- How many different types of insects are there?
- Where do insects live?

- How do insects help other animals and people? What jobs do they do?
- How many legs do insects have?
- Do all insects have wings?
- What do insects eat?
- What animals eat insects?
- How many insects can you name?
- What's your favourite bug?

Turn the page to add some notes to the journal space. There are some extra journal pages at the back of the book too.

What did I find today?

TODO IS ....

WHERE AM I?...

Draw something here

Draw a bug you saw

What can you smell?

What was the colour of the sky?

Stick a leaf here!

| 3 |

WALK THREE

Frame it, Squash it, Bash it!

TIME: 30 MINUTES TO 2 HOURS
THEME: FLORA
LOCATION: STREET, PARK, GARDEN, WOODS

Did you know that spending time outdoors can boost creativity? Stepping away from screens and into any kind of outdoor space enables our minds to open up to new experiences. This can be boosted by taking a stroll with enough time to allow our minds and thoughts to wander. Noticing new things, experiencing new places or asking each other interesting questions helps our brains to make creative connections.

In a natural environment, we tend to allow our thoughts to be bigger and leave ourselves room to be inspired. Our mood gets a little extra lift from being outdoors, especially when we are surrounded by

green. When we feel in a positive mood, our attention is broader and we notice more. Just being in nature can inspire us. The dew drops on a spider web, patterns in tree bark or on a leaf, the hundreds of colours on flowers or insects.

Making can be a joyful experience for kids and even more fun when we give permission to get mucky and do things we wouldn't usually do, like bash up a leaf to make a picture. And that's exactly what we'll be doing in this walk. We will take time to notice how creative nature can be in its colours, shapes and forms. On the way, we will make 3 nature-based artworks of our own!

What you'll need

The homemade playdough activity sheet
- download from wildkidsaustralia.com.au/naturesnotscary

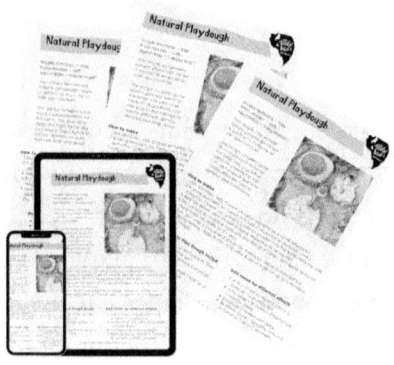

Extra things to take with you in your nature adventure backpack:

- Extra string (natural jute or hessian is best)

- Chunky crayons
- Paper
- Camera or phone
- Container for collecting flowers and leaves
- Homemade playdough (see notes below)
- Clean up cloths, water or wipes for mucky hands

Frame it, squash it, bash it - snapshot

- The walk includes 3 nature-based art activities.
- Frame it - make a stick frame for your own art
- Squash it - Make a face on a tree and copy the bark pattern
- Bash it - Create your own paints using flowers and leaves
- Plan a walk that will take at least 30 minutes.
- Aim to walk in an area that has trees and flowering, leafy plants.
- Download the activity sheet.
- The activity pack includes instructions for making your own playdough.
- If you plan to use playdough you'll need to make this before your walk (see the instructions for the 'squash it' activity for details).

Here are three activities to frame it, squash it and bash it on your walk

1. **Frame it!**
   The first activity couldn't be simpler. Find 4 sturdy sticks to tie together to make a frame! You can make this any size you like. Using sticks around 30cm - 40cm each is a good starter. Be sure to use string that is reasonably thick, and has some grip to it. Natural hessian is perfect. Place your sticks on a flat surface in a square or rectangular frame shape so the ends slightly overlap. Starting with one corner, wrap the string in a figure 8 motion so that the first 2 sticks are firmly secured. Then, tie the other sticks

on until you have a strong shape. Your stick frame is perfect for so many activities while you're out and about. You can try....

- Hanging it from a tree for photo opportunities (see also the next activity)
- Placing it on the ground to see what nature you can find in the square
- Putting natural treasures that you find inside it, then draw or photograph your 'scene'.

2. **Squash it!**

Taking a walk in the woods, your local park or street to choose a favourite tree is a great start to engaging kids in discussions about all the different trees that nature has created and exploring patterns in nature. In this activity, we will be making a face on our favourite tree.

Find a sturdy tree that has a trunk wide enough for a good-sized face. Trees with quite rough, knobbly bark work best for this activity as smooth bark is a bit slippery (a good experiment to try though!). The base for your tree face can be clay, playdough or simple mud. Be sure to choose something that is toxin-free. Natural, homemade playdough is perfect and you can download our activity pack for our tried and tested recipe. If you decide you'd rather make your own mud, aim for a sticky thick consistency. Kids have extra fun with this part! We suggest taking a bottle of water and washcloths with you to clean up afterwards.

Begin by squishing some clay or mud onto the tree to make some eyes, nose and mouth shapes. Then explore the local area for some interesting items to add to the face. Perhaps a pine cone for a nose, or stick mouth. Push the different pieces firmly into the clay on the tree to decorate.

Some kids find getting mucky a bit challenging and encouraging with permission and excitement with the creative task helps to support them learning through this experience. You might want to lead by example and get a bit dirty too! The advantage of making a mud face is that you can leave the face there until nature takes it back into the ground again. Use the stick frame you made earlier to frame your tree face as you take a picture.

3. **Bash it!**

Rather than use paints in plastic tubs, experiment with flower-bashing pictures. This activity is fantastic for coordination and talking about risk-tasking when using tools. As well as producing beautiful results! Gather some colourful flowers and leaves.

Place them on a piece of thick paper and bash them with a hammer or stone onto the paper. As you bash, the colour from the flowers and leaves transfers onto the paper and you are left with a beautiful painting. Take care with little fingers while bashing. This activity presents a good opportunity to talk about safety while using tools. You can help younger children get used to the motion first to build confidence. Choosing quite fleshy flowers or leaves with bright colours gets the best results.

Conversation starters

When you're out and about on your frame it, squash it, bash it walk, there are so many conversations that we can begin to encourage that curious creativity.

- What can you see in the frame? How many plants or insects?
- How does the stick feel? Is it bumpy or smooth?
- Which one is your favourite tree? Why?

- How many different types of tree can you see?
- Why are some leaves wide and broad, and some are thin and narrow?
- Do you see different colours in the tree leaves?
- What does the mud or playdough feel like?
- Which flower is the brightest? The darkest? The biggest or smallest?
- Why are flowers different colours?
- What colour will this flower make on the paper? What about this leaf?

Turn the page to add some notes to the journal space. There are some extra journal pages at the back of the book too.

What did I find today?

TODAY IS ....

WHERE AM I?..

Draw something here

Draw a bug you saw

What can you smell?

What was the colour of the sky?

Stick a leaf here!

| 4 |

WALK FOUR

Stick Den Adventure

TIME: 60 MINUTES TO ALL DAY
THEME: HABITAT
LOCATION: HOUSE, GARDEN, BALCONY, PARK, WOODS

Some of my happiest memories are of being curled up on a cushion, in the torchlight, in my very own made den. My construction methods were chairs, blankets, sheets and cushions. The odd peg here and there for design enhancement and perhaps a broom for additional structure. I took my den building seriously! And I remember how proud I was that I had created my own dwelling. A space that was only mine. Hidden from the rest of the house.

Even better was when we ventured out to the woods to make a proper stick den. Those days were super adventurous. Finding the right location, searching for sticks that were the best fit, and looking for leafy branches to make the roof. And then hiding out. Although it was often not as comfy as the living room dens, the sense of achievement was greater because I'd made it outside.

In a den building activity, we can discuss shape and structure as well as what kinds of architecture or materials work. That sounds technical, but really it's all about figuring out things like needing strong sturdy sticks to hold up the smaller leafy sticks of your walls and roof, so it doesn't fall in. You can practice safe ways of breaking, playing with and carrying sticks. Trying out these techniques on a small scale is a safer option. And it's much more accessible because you only need a few short sticks, some decorative bits and a small space. If you have a garden or can access a park or woodland, then this mini den-building activity works well outside. Bringing the materials inside for an indoor den is just as much fun.

On this walk, we will create a sense of achievement and pride as we build our own stick dens. We start small with a den for our favourite toy. Then we can get bigger with a child-sized or even family-sized den. We will also play a game to match the animal to their tree home.

What you'll need

Match the animal and home activity - download from wildkidsaustralia.com.au/naturesnotscary

Extra things to take with you in your nature adventure backpack:

- Old sheet
- Picnic blanket
- Soft stuffed animal or favourite toy
- Extra string, thick enough to tie sticks

Stick den adventure - Snapshot

- You'll be building a den and collecting the materials your need on your walk!
- The activity pack includes a fun card-matching game to play at home or in your den. The game prompts conversations about animal habitats.
- When you are planning your walk remember to choose an area where you will be able to collect some fallen sticks and leaves for building materials.
- If you are new to den building, start with a small toy-sized den. Once you are confident you can build a person-sized den.
- Choose one of the 3 main den building designs explained in this chapter:
    - Tripod
    - Lean-to

○ Burrow

A toy-sized den

Start by making a mini-sized stick den for your favourite toy. The perfect introduction to den building. Collect the sticks as you walk along and then find a flat spot to build on. Check the area to make sure there is nothing bitey, stingy or scratchy before you start!

A person-sized den

The only difference with a person-sized den is that you will need bigger sticks! And you need to make sure that the den is safely tied together so that it doesn't fall in unexpectedly. Choose from the 3 different den types in this chapter and start with your frame, tying some strong sticks together. Test each join for strength and wobble it a bit to test even more. Test it out to see if you can sit or stand up inside. Once you are happy, start to layer on your smaller sticks and leaves. Pop a cozy blanket and some cushions on the floor. The perfect space to play the habitat matching game (see the download link in this chapter). And of course, there are so many cute photo opportunities :)

Note: Please only collect sticks or leaves that have already fallen from the tree or bush. Please do not cut or break living branches or plants. When you have finished playing with your den, return the sticks so the bugs, fungus and mosses can enjoy them!

Here are three easy-to-make den structures to try

1. **Tripod**

    Find 3 or 5 quite sturdy sticks and lean them towards each other to make a simple cone shape. It's helpful with this type of structure to use some string to tie the tops of the sticks. This provides a firm base and is great for beginner den builders, as it's less likely to collapse while building. Add some lighter twiggy, leafy sticks around the outside of the structure to form the walls. Leave one section clear for the entrance, and you're done! If you're building this den inside, then using a soft blanket as a base gives a good texture for the sticks to sit on without slipping down.

2. **Lean-to**

   If you don't have string handy then the simple lean-to den is a perfect introduction to den building and super simple. Particularly useful in a woodland setting. First, find something to form your main structure and to 'lean' all the other sticks on to. This can be a log, a wall, a box or a strong stick. Collect some twigs and sticks and lean them all along one side of your main support. You'll end up with a triangle-shaped den with 'doors' at both ends. Lay some leafy sticks on top to make it extra cosy.

3. **Burrow**

   If you want to get a bit more adventurous with your den design, you can progress to making a burrow with a curved structure. These take a little more time, but the end result is super cute and there is a huge sense of achievement in creating a more complex design. For this type of den, you'll need to collect some curved sticks to form the main structure. Arrange the curved sticks in a dome or tunnel shape, crossing over each other to form a strong frame. Use some thinner curved sticks to lay on top, crisis crossing as you go. Finish with leafy sticks or thin pieces of bark. It's fun to add something soft inside to make a snuggly nest.

Conversation starters

During the building process and once you've made the den and you and/or your toy are comfortably settled in, there are so many conversations that we can centre around this activity.

- What is your favourite thing about your shelter?
- What would you do differently next time? What worked well?
- What would you like to add? Or take away?
- What kinds of homes do animals live in?
- What kind of animal lives in a burrow?
- What kind of animal lives in a tree?
- How would your den feel in the summer? or winter?
- Could you build a person-sized den too?
- What kinds of homes do people live in? Where it is hot or cold? Now and in the past?

Turn the page to add some notes to the journal space. There are some extra journal pages at the back of the book too.

What did I find today?

TODAY IS ....

WHERE AM I? ....

Draw something here

Draw a bug you saw

What can you smell?

What was the colour of the sky?

Stick a leaf here!

| 5 |

WALK FIVE

Whether it's Sunny or Not

TIME: 30 MINUTES TO 2 HOURS
THEME: CLIMATE
LOCATION: CITY, PARK, GARDEN, WOODS - ANYWHERE CLOSE TO HOME

Young children grasp most weather concepts easily. They have had splashy experiences of wet rainy days and seen raindrops falling from clouds. They will have felt the warm sunshine on their skin and seen the sun in the sky. A thunder and lightning storm may have excited them. They might have felt a snowflake melt on their hand. Or seen the after-effects of a hailstorm.

From these early experiences, we can expand their understanding of how weather creates a rhythm for the natural world and governs all living things. We can discuss weather conditions over a day, week or month and talk about seasons. The best way for children to grasp seasonal changes is to repeat a walk in a similar area at different times and discuss the changes you see from month to month.

In the area where you live there may be dramatic seasonal changes. Like leaves falling from trees so they are bare in winter and full in summer. You may have icy temperatures with heavy snowfall followed by hot summers. Or in more tropical zones the changes might be more subtle but may include a rainy season. Discussing changes in weather over time introduces the idea of climate and from there a conversation about climate change. There is an opportunity to discuss the weather and climate knowledge of first nations people in the area you live. In some locations, for example, Europeans introduced the four seasons that occur in northern Europe whereas the traditional owners described 6 different seasons that are more accurate for local conditions. Check the resources section at the end of this book for more information.

What you'll need

The weather station activity pack
- download from wildkidsaustralia.com.au/naturesnotscary

Extra things to take with you in your nature adventure backpack

- Paper
- Collecting bag

- Camera

Whether its sunny or not - Snapshot

- This walk is all about different kinds of weather and how climate impacts our environment.
- Choose a short walk ideally at a time with changeable weather like spring or autumn so that you can experience different weather conditions.
- When you are planning your walk remember that you will want to come back to the same location to record your weather observations, so somewhere close to home, even our own backyard is best.
- Download the activity pack.
- The activity pack includes step-by-step instructions to make your own weather monitoring station and a weather recording logbook.
- The activity ideas include making leaf shadow puppets on sunny days and upcycled wind chimes for windy days.
- Repeat the walk a few times in the space of a week or even a month.

1. **Set up a weather monitoring station**

    If there is one thing that we know it's that the weather changes. Sometimes it can be predicted and sometimes it takes everyone by surprise. But it's always changing. And that's great because there are fun experiments we can do outside, whether it's sunny or not!

    For this activity, we will be making a weather monitoring station from repurposed rubbish. In the activity sheet that you can download using the link above, there are full instructions for making your weather monitoring station. Once you have made your weather monitoring station you can take it with you on your next walk or pop it in an area that is exposed to the weather in your garden or balcony. You can use the weather recording logbook from the activity pack to note changes in measurements and weather conditions on different walks and at different times.

2. **Create a leaf shadow puppet**

On a sunny day, we can make some cool shadow puppets on our walk. As you walk, collect some interesting shaped leaves that have fallen to the ground. A clear, crisp Autumn day is a great time for this. Set a piece of paper down in a bright spot and hold the leaves up above the paper to cast shadows. What shapes can you see and make? Does the shadow get larger or smaller the closer it is to the paper? Try tying some leaves and sticks together to make people, animals or crazy creature shapes - use your imagination! Hold a leaf up to make the shadow and draw around the shadow to 'trace' the leaf.

3. **Repurpose junk to make some wind chimes**

Wind can be a tricky topic to explain to kids. We can't see the wind itself, but we can see the effects it has on the trees, for example, feel a cool or warm breeze or smell scents carried by it.

It's also a big concept to explain where it comes from because the wind is made on a global scale. The sun heats air which rises, cools and falls. The rotation of the earth then twists and turns the air which creates complex wind patterns.

We can introduce the concept of wind with fun activities that use the wind like paper kites. We can discuss how plants use the wind to blow their leaves off, blow down old trees or spread their seeds. And also, how people use wind for travel, industry and creating energy.

A fun way to demonstrate the effects of wind is by repurposing some rubbish to make upcycled wind chimes! Use a cardboard ice cream or coffee cup and poke a hole in the top. Thread through some thick string. Tie a loop in one end for hanging and secure the other end by tying a few knots so it doesn't slip back through the hole. Then poke some holes around the rim of the cup. Thread different lengths of string thorough and attach some sticks that you collected on your walk and/or old plastic bottle tops. Make sure the sticks hang close enough to know together when the cup sways in the breeze. Hang up on a tree or outside on your balcony and wait for the wind to make some tunes!

Conversation starters

On your weather walk, you might start some conversations about the weather with these questions.

- How does the sun feel on your skin?
- Does the rain feel cold or warm?
- What does the sun make us feel like doing?
- What does the cold make us feel like doing?
- What kinds of weather are useful for people to use? For energy? For transport? To make food?
- What fun things can we do when it's windy?
- What does a storm feel, look and sound like?
- What happens to plants and animals when it is hot?
- What is rain? Why do we need rain?
- What happens when we have too much sun, or too much rain? What about not enough?
- When do birds make nests?
- When do flowers bloom the most?

Turn the page to add some notes to the journal space. There are some extra journal pages at the back of the book too.

What did I find today?

TODAY IS ....

WHERE AM I?..

Draw something here

Draw a bug you saw

What can you smell?

What was the colour of the sky?

Stick a leaf here!

| 6 |

WALK SIX

Make Your Own Way

TIME: 30 - 60 MINUTES (PLUS PREP TIME)
THEME: SUSTAINABILITY
LOCATION: ANY LOCATION WITH A PATH - YOUR LOCAL BLOCK, STREET, PARK OR WOODS

What gives us the motivation to look after our environment? A sense of connection to the place we live is what makes us care about looking after it. We can have conversations about reducing, reusing and recycling but unless we actually care about protecting our home there isn't the motivation to keep us doing it. A sense of belonging is important for young children. It connects them to the place they live, the people that are close to them and the people they meet every day. The familiarity of a tree, a flowering shrub, birds singing in the morning, and a favourite hedge that has a nice smell all connect us to our local area. And the connection supports the idea that conservation of the natural environment and sustainability of our surrounding matters to everyone.

Nurturing a sense of belonging for children is especially important for their well-being too. In fact, studies have shown that children who feel a sense of belonging at school do better both emotionally and academically. We can support this by encouraging knowledge of our local area and a connection with our community.

In this walk, we will make our own nature trail. We will build those connections between ourselves, the place we live and the people we share our lives with. We can even involve family, friends or our local neighbourhood. This is a great confidence builder and is vital for overall well-being as well as motivating us to want to take care of our home, our community and the planet.

What you'll need

The nature trail activity pack
- download from wildkidsaustralia.com.au/naturesnotscary

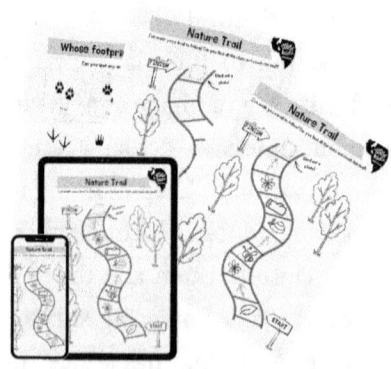

To prepare your trail
- Pebbles
- Paint
- Glue

Extra things to take with you in your nature adventure backpack
- The nature trail map (from the activity pack)
- Your nature trail pebble markers
- Camera

Make your own way - Snapshot
- This walk is all about connecting with our local area and community.
- Choose a short walk - ideally one that will be easily accessible for friends and family.
- You'll be making your own nature trail, using pebble markers that you will make by painting at home.
- Download the activity pack.
- The activity pack includes a trail map example, plus one that you can use to make your own.
- The activity pack also includes a fun bonus activity to spot animal tracks.
- Paint your pebble markers using the designs on the example trail or with your own designs.
- Place your pebbles to mark the trail.
- Share the trail map with friends and family and ask them to send you a photo when they reach the end of the trail.

Here is how to create your very own nature trail!

1. **Make your markers**

    To make our nature trail we need to be able to mark our way at different points along the track. And then record them in the order we should find them on our trail map. The aim is to make it easy for us to repeat our steps, and to be able to share the trail with others so they can follow the trail too. Before we head out on our walk, we need to make our markers. Pebbles work really well for this because they will stay in place without blowing away. Choose pebbles that are large enough to paint on and be seen clearly. Use the symbols on the example activity trail that's in the downloadable pack, or choose your own and paint a pebble with one design each. Before you start painting you may need to seal the stone with a thin coat of glue and allow it to dry. Use paint that doesn't wash off easily or seal the paint once it's dry with another coat of glue. Leave the pebbles to dry for at least 24 hours before heading out on your walk.

2. **Create your trail**

    Choose a walk that's quite close to home, that has a clear path (ideally with a couple of places where it twists, turns or forks) and that is accessible to friends and family. Head out on your walk with your pebble markers that you made in step 1. Don't forget to take your trail map with you. Decide where you would like the trail to start and place your first marker pebble at that place. A good position is clearly visible from the path but out of the way enough so it won't be disturbed. Take a photo of the start of the trail. Place the rest of your markers along the path in the same order as your trail map. Choose interesting locations not too far apart. You can also make some arrow shapes with sticks to mark the direction. On the way, talk about what you can hear, see, smell and touch. Take notice of big and small things. What nature lives here? What nature comes and goes in the day? Or at night? Who lives here? Can you find any animal tracks? When you reach the end of your trail place your last marker and take a picture of the area.

3. **Share your trail**

   It's time to challenge your friends and family to follow your trail. Share the trail map with them and your photo of the start. Ask them to follow the markers and find their way to the finish. You can ask them to send you a photo of the end of the trail. For added fun, you could offer a prize to whoever completes the trail first. Or share the trail with your school class for them to follow. Why not go with some family members and watch them try to find your markers - don't give them any clues though!

Conversation starters

On your nature trail walk or while you're making your pebble markers, you might start some conversations about looking after the place we live with these questions.

- What is your favourite thing about our street? Near our house?
- Where is your favourite place to play outside near home?
- Who else lives near our home?
- What is it like where your family live? Nearby or far away?
- How do we know which way to walk to school? To the shops? To a friend's house?
- What tells us the way on a path or road?
- What nature do you see on your way to the shops? School? Park?
- Who else plays in the park?
- What animals live in or visit the park? Can you find their footprints?
- How do we find our way to the park?
- Should we look after our home? Our street? Our area?
- Do we throw rubbish on the ground where we live?

- How else can we look after our home? Animal homes?

Turn the page to add some notes to the journal space. There are some extra journal pages at the back of the book too.

What did I find today?

TODAY IS ....

WHERE AM I?..

Draw something here

Draw a bug you saw

What can you smell?

What was the colour of the sky?

Stick a leaf here!

NATURE JOURNAL PAGES

My Nature Journal

Wild kids AUSTRALIA

Record what you find on your next adventure in nature!

TODAY IS........................

WHAT CAN I SEE?

WHERE AM I TODAY?

WHAT KIND OF PLACE IS IT?

- [ ] FOREST?
- [ ] PARK?
- [ ] GARDEN?
- [ ]
- [ ] BEACH?
- [ ] STREET?
- [ ] POND OR STREAM?
- [ ]

tick something here

What did I find?

WHAT DID I FIND?

- [ ]
- [ ]
- [ ]
- [ ]
- [ ]
- [ ]
- [ ]

WHAT'S ON THE GROUND?

WHAT'S UP ABOVE?

HOW MANY BUGS DID I SPOT?

MY FAVOURITE BUG TODAY

Splodge something here

What has changed?

WHAT ELSE DO I WANT TO REMEMBER?

WHAT'S DIFFERENT FROM THE LAST TIME I WAS HERE?

DO A LEAF, STONE OR BARK RUBBING HERE

WHAT DO I FEEL HERE?

extra notes?

WHAT ELSE DO I WANT TO REMEMBER?

....
....
....
....
....
....
....
....
....

STICK SOMETHING HERE

DRAW SOMETHING HERE

What did I find today?

TODO IS ....

WHERE AM I? ....

MAKE YOU OWN OBSERVATION KIT

Observing wildlife can be tricky. Especially when it comes to things that move quickly or are far away. If you're taking a look at a bug, an old jar works well. Just place the jar over the top of the bug to keep it in one place long enough to examine it. The glass will help magnify a little. Be sure to let the bug go after a few minutes.

Your local market, vintage shop or second-hand store might hold interesting items like binoculars or magnifying glasses. Great for examining up close or investigating far away. You might also pick up some interesting second-hand books about animals and plants in your area.

If you've discovered some tiny bugs on your walk, a homemade pooter is a great way to take a closer look! A bug pooter is a small, handheld device that is used to suck up bugs. Pooters are easy to make at home and are fun to put together.

Note: You'll be using some tools and sharp objects so this is an adult-led activity.

Homemade bug pooter

What you'll need
- A clean jar (an old spice/herb jar is perfect),
- Plastic tubing (about 70cm),

- A 10cm square piece of muslin or similar (old stockings fabric is perfect)
- An elastic band (repurpose one from a recent veggie purchase)
- A nail and a hammer.
- A sharp craft knife.

How to make

1. Punch 2 holes in the lid of your jar. A nail and hammer work well for this. Wear gloves in case you slip.
2. Using a sharp knife make the holes large enough to pop your tubing through. The tubing should fit snugly.
3. Cut a 40cm length of the tube and pop it through one of the holes, threading about 6cm through. Take the remaining piece of tube and thread it through the other hole. Fold your piece of muslin or stocking fabric over the end of the shorter tube and wrap it around the elastic band so that it's tight.
4. Screw the lid onto the jar and it's done!
5. Top tip: The covered muslin tube end should be inside the jar.

  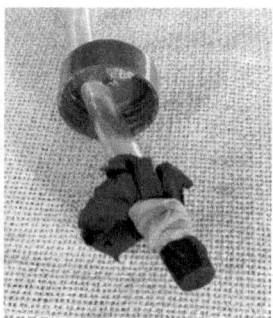

Instructions for use

To use your pooter, place your mouth over the tube that has the covered end. And the other tube end over a bug. Breathe in and the bug will be sucked up into the jar! Don't worry - the fabric covering inside the jar on the end of the breathing jube will stop you from being able to breathe in the bug. Once in the jar, you can use the magnification of the glass to get a closer look before releasing your bug back to its home.

Wildkids Trevor using a pooter

RISK ASSESSMENT

When you go for a nature adventure walk with your children, it's important to do a risk assessment first. This simply means that you think about what could go wrong and how you can prevent it or deal with it. For example, if you're going to walk in the woods, you might want to be careful about where you step because there might be bugs or animals that could make you sick. You might want to take a first aid kit with some sting-soothing lotion in it for insect bites. If you're going to the beach, you may need to tell your children about staying safe near the water.

A risk assessment can be as simple as a checklist. Here are a few things to keep in mind when thinking about risks.

First, consider the activity you're planning and the potential hazards involved. Will you be exploring near a body of water? Using tools? If so, proper supervision and safety precautions will be necessary.

Next, consider the age and abilities of your kids. Some activities may be too challenging or dangerous for younger children, while others may be easy for older children. Think about where you will be walking. If it's close to home, then the risks may be minimal. Further afield or in a remote area that you've never been to before, you may need to think more carefully.

Finally, don't forget to factor in the weather. High winds, extreme heat or cold, and slippery conditions can all increase the risk of injury, especially for young children. By taking these factors into account, you can ensure a safe and enjoyable experience for everyone involved.

Remember that children are pretty good at assessing risk for themselves. They tend not to climb a tree much higher than they can manage, for example. You know your kids best. What their capabilities are and what you should discuss with them. We don't need to discuss all of the risks we may consider as adults. This may only increase anxiety for some. But you may wish to gently introduce the idea of some potential hazards for them to manage. Not picking berries from plants would be a useful example.

The most important thing to remember is that being prepared is the best safety measure. Once you've ticked that off your list - go have some mucky, adventurous fun!

Consider these steps when creating your risk assessment checklist:

- Consider the activity and potential hazards involved
- Take into account the age and abilities of the children and adults
- Factor in the weather conditions
- Consider how children will be supervised at all times
- Provide safety and or weather gear as necessary
- Have a basic first aid kit on hand
- Create an emergency plan.

A simple checklist for a walk in the park might include:

- Check the weather conditions and dress appropriately
- Think through potential dangers and what to do if you encounter them
- Make sure children are supervised at all times
- Stay on marked trails

- Consider whether the area has clear boundaries or fences, clear paths
- Watch for poisonous plants, insects, and animals
- Be aware of surroundings and potential hazards
- Check your adventure backpack for supplies

About the author

Rachel Abel is an experienced educator and leadership development specialist who has dedicated her career to positive social change.

She's worked in senior roles in Education, Government and Health for over 30 years. A leadership coach and university educator, Rachel is co-founder of Wildkids Australia, a business that delivers nature and education resources.

With a deep love for the natural world, Rachel believes that everyone deserves to experience its wonder and beauty, now and in the future. Rachel's passion for nature began when she was young, and she has spent her life exploring the outdoors. This, along with her career experience. has given her a unique perspective on the importance of nature and sustainability education. Rachel currently lives in Sydney, Australia, with her husband and two young children. When she's not butterfly watching, investigating moss on an old log, teaching, writing, baking or spending time with her family, you can be sure to find her in, on or next to the ocean. Rachel is excited to share her knowledge and hopes to inspire others to continue their nature adventures!

Then and now - Rachel in one of her stick and blanket dens circa 1979, and more recently amongst her houseplants!

ADDITIONAL RESOURCES

Atchley RA, Strayer DL, Atchley P (2012) Creativity in the Wild: Improving Creative Reasoning through Immersion in Natural Settings. PLoS ONE

Beery T, Jørgensen KA (2018) Children in nature: sensory engagement and the experience of biodiversity, Environmental Education Research, 24:1, 13-25

Dankiw KA, Tsiros MD, Baldock KL, Kumar S (2020) The impacts of unstructured nature play on health in early childhood development: A systematic review.

Kemple KM, Oh J, Kenney E, Smith-Bonahue T (2016) The Power of Outdoor Play and Play in Natural Environments, Childhood Education, 92:6, 446-454

Sobel, D., 2014. Place-Based Education: Connecting Classrooms and Communities. Closing the Achievement Gap: The SEER Report. *NAMTA Journal, 39*(1), pp.61-78.

www.ingramcontent.com/pod-product-compliance
Lightning Source LLC
Chambersburg PA
CBHW070311010526
44107CB00056B/2562